Dances with Vowels

For the two Dots.

Dances with Vowels
Poems by Kevin Cadwallender

STACK
BOOKS

Published 2009 by
Smokestack Books
PO Box 408, Middlesbrough TS5 6WA
e-mail : info@smokestack-books.co.uk
www.smokestack-books.co.uk

Dances with Vowels
Kevin Cadwallender
Cover photo: Alan Sill.
Hands: Anne Musgrove.

Printed by
EPW Print & Design Ltd

ISBN 978-0-9554028-6-9
Smokestack Books gratefully
acknowledges the support of
Middlesbrough Borough Council
and Arts Council North East

Smokestack Books is
represented by Inpress Ltd
www.inpressbooks.co.uk

Contents

Workhorse

So they spat you
Out to pension,
Carved your name in
That last seam of coal.
The air coughed black
As you wretched your
Lungs to a standstill.

Owners receive
Reward for exploitation,
Count each tick on the hands
Of their presentation clocks.
Your hands were hard
And scarred by work.
I can feel them now
Rough and gentle
On my skin.

Regardless, they are pulling
The colliery down.
And I turn to you,
Demolished in
This hospital bed.

And Then There's Dallas

And then there's *Dallas*
Full of cars, big cigars
Big buxom women
With big buxom psychiatric problems,
And then there's J.R
With his bloody silly hats
All that money and he can't afford a decent hat.

It's a conspiracy you know
The Americans never liked us
Cos we just drive sensible cars
And call soccer football
And then we had the Beatles
And they only had the Monkees
And one of them were English.

I don't watch it like
Cos I'm an intellectual
I watch *Panorama, Tomorrow's World*
Don't understand them but that's beside the point
I mean there's no realism in *Dallas*
Dallas load of crap
Give me *Crossroads* or *Coronation Street*
anytime.

Under Capricorn

She said, 'Aren't the stars beautiful'
He explained the gasses in their make-up,
           Their distance from him, gave
           The latin name for each star,
           Their constellation and magnitude.
She said, 'I could reach up
           And put one in my pocket'
He smiled, and explained the difference in circumference
           Between Sirius and her pocket, went on
           To explain how stars evolve, how stars die
She listened to his voice
           Nodded her acquiescence
           And not wanting to disturb his world,
           Emptied her pockets
                        Of stars.

Paradise Lost

We were never
Ones for Paradise,
If I gave you
An apple you'd
Only eat it.
And our naked
Majesty, no doubt,
Would be marred
By your stretch
Marks and my paunch.

So it's best to
Stick to what we know,
I'm not keen on gardening
And Eden would soon
Be overgrown.

Let Paradise stay lost,
Only look to find us,
Falling all the way
To Heaven.

Concentrate

'Concentrate', he said,
'If we all concentrate
            we can change the world',
So we concentrated,
All over the world
people stopped everything
and concentrated.
            In bedsits, the walls clammy with thought,
                        young lovers concentrated,
                        if only on each other.
            In dole queues people swayed silently,
                        thinking away unemployment.
            In third world countries, starving children
                        linked minds with millionaires
                        and brought an end to famine.
'Concentrate', he said.
            In the East and West top level concentration
                        brought an end to the arms race,
            The government brought in legislation,
                        levied taxes on trains of thought,
                        Concentration camps were opened
                        in every social security office.
People gathered for think-ins, the arts council organised
      think festivals,
The army went on manoeuvres in think tanks.
'Concentrate', he said.
      The Thinker became a symbol of salvation,
      Socrates was made a saint,
      Everyone thought therefore they were,
      Poets became a thing of the past,
      The most valuable substance on earth
      became the human brain,
      Capitalists organised brain banks,
      The poor became brain donors,
      Thought became the domain of the wealthy.
'Concentrate', he said,
As he closed his wallet.

Off the Beaten Tract

Off the beaten tract
Karl Marx doing Walt Whitman impressions,
tucks his beard into his 501's
squares up to a cash dispenser.

PLEASE KEY IN YOUR PIN.
1 – 8 – 1 – 8

(Feel the silicon shift
in the Rhineland synagogue.)

WHICH SERVICE DO YOU REQUIRE?

Balance?

Feel the discontent
seething in the dusty words
bubbling under the British Museum.
How can there ever be balance?

NO BALANCE AVAILABLE.

(How can there be a balance?)

DO YOU REQUIRE ANOTHER SERVICE?

Man cannot live by plastic alone
the middle classes croon
to mortgaged love songs.
Keeping up the instalments
on Time's Winged Chariot.

PLEASE REMOVE YOUR CARD COMPLETELY.

Off the beaten tract
to the *Das Kapital* Winebar
Karl Marx
ordering two red flags with ice.

At Some Point in Time We Fractured

At some point in time we fractured,
uncertain of which bones to break
we broke them all,
climbed walls
without fear
of falling
At some point in time we fractured,
uncertain of which promises to break
we broke our own,
and being unable to keep broken promises,
we made new ones,

Not all the king's horses,
nor all the king's men
have our vanity.

This Winter the Angles Were All Wrong

This winter the angles were all wrong,
Light did not cut the darkness in its usual way.
And your embrace was calculated
as though you were aware
of the emphasis being changed.

Time has broken out of its confines,
Clockfaces turn against us,
The roses are latticed
and climb in oblique strategy.

Winter's fractured bones
consecrate shadows,
I watch you as your lips
move out of synch,
uttering syllables
of half-lost songs.

This winter the angles were all wrong,
You denied the existence of corners,
as if something of startling originality
could be wrought by denial.

I am losing you by degrees.

Clocks

These minutes with you
are measured by the clock.

Clocks don't give a fuck.
and time we spend
in making love
or waking with children
is captured
in segments of
luminous green
on black.
Clocks have no propriety,
I lie listening to
our love ticking
and dream of
a genocide of
clocks.

Superman

Superman shops in a supermarket,
Buys all-american beans,
no artificial additives,
no immigrant glutamates,
low in cholesterol
100% red-necked mainstream beans,
Good for the digestion,
No kryptonite in these boys,
Fart like a skyscraper
Pebble-dash clouds.

The man of steel is an alien!
and you all know what aliens do,
You've read *War of the Worlds*,
You've seen *Invasion of the Bodysnatchers* -
It's in their blood!
Does Superman bleed?
Does Superman use Superglue?
If Superman is superstitious
What does 'stitious' mean?

Not that I'm against aliens,
Some of my best friends haven't
been on this planet for years.
But a man of steel is a sexist icon,
Is the American dream in its underwear,
And don't you find it strange
that in all that overwhelming vastness of stars
we should get lumbered with a white male
English speaking democrat who just happens
to land in the USA?
Suspicious is not the word (well it is actually)

Anyway I don't trust him
and if he wasn't a fictitious character
I'd tell him to his face.

Table Manners

'A penis,'
she said,
to invited guests,
'is a sensitive, solitary
creature, with a mind suited
to only one thing.'

The blue vein
throbbed in
her temple.
'I have encountered many
in my younger years
which stood not
the test of time.'

'Bollocks',
I countered,
'Make a lovely couple'

The table was set
for sex.

Magritte Reflecting Dali

The day Rene Magritte
unstuck the bird from his face,
Was the day I came unglued.
Cuckoos melted over metal branches,
The pavement perspired
I looked into a mirror
And saw a mirror.
I went into the kitchen
to prise the narcissi
from my eggs,
to find Frenchmen
injecting houses
with sky.
The day Rene Magritte
unstuck the bird from his face
was the day I came unglued.
I looked at my reflection
in a bowl of water,
I saw an elephant
and knew the truth,
I glided out of the kitchen
in search of Leda.

Life on Mars

It was a god-awful small affair,
Nothing to break into xenophobia about,
A girl with mousy hair
and the boy next door from Mars.

And it's got to be better
than cavemen fighting in dance halls.
And it's got to be better than
out of focus cinematic Iberian mice.

It was after all the best selling show,
I loved the blackness of her skin
and her father hated me for being green
and out of work.

And who would have
suspected Mickey Mouse
of bovine tendencies
and who would have thought
Britannia would start the revolution without us.

I loved the quaint earth gravity
of her conversation,
She liked my sense of humour
though she never really got the one
about my Mother, the dog and clowns
though it had them rolling in the aisles
on the red planet.

We could have gone places
there was a whole universe out there
just begging for exploration,
but she liked her home comforts too much,
Men with only one head, gravity, oxygen
and god-awful small affairs
are doomed
when mousy haired girls
and green men
run out of conversation.

Chez Machismo

So you're a house husband?
He said this like Arthur Scargill
Used to say, *So you're a scab!*
I asked him to tell me what
He understood by house husband
And he fair leered
Do you do all the things
that a woman is supposed to do?
And I said,
Well I wouldn't fuck you
So yes! I suppose I do.
And he went puce
And started ranting on about
Not being a shirt lifter
And he called me names
That he never said in front of his wife
And he smacked me in the mouth
So I belted him in the eye
Which meant that we had to
Go to the match together
And shout abuse at referees
And do a foursome at Pizza Hut
And we did that for years
Until his wife left him for
Another woman and he stopped
Speaking to me when I called him
A blouse for crying in public.

Me and the Racist Next Door

Me and the racist next door
are going out drinking,
celebrating his bigotry
revelling in his intolerance
and when he's drunk enough
I am going to kill him.

Listen,
The racist next door is
making jokes about the 'darkies'
and the 'half-chats' and the 'gypos'
He is laughing at his own one track wit'
Tonight is his special night,
Come on down Racist bastard!
For when he has filled me with his hatred
I am going to vent his ideology with an axe.

The racist next door
with his white smug wife
is calling my wife a black bitch,
Is ranting and raving with
the full force of his Ordinary level brain,
He does not understand words like 'dogmatism'
He does not understand.
He does not understand when my wife
calls him an arsehole in Bengali,
He has no capacity to comprehend.

Tonight I will speak to him in his language,
It is a tongue easily learned,
It is a tongue I used in my youth,
Tonight I will use violence
to communicate with him.

Me and the racist next door
are going to paint the town red.

Going Native

Walking amidst a profusion of flora and fauna.
How d'yer turn that into poetry?
Everyone knows Flora is polyunsaturated margarine.
Anyways I wandered bemused as fuck
through cascades of purple flowers
You know the ones I mean?
Them big Spiky ones,
Scotland's full of them,
at least I think they're flowers!
Could be. I'm no Botanist mind.

Listening to the beautiful song of...er...
Y'know them little brown birds,
The ones poets go on about all the time,
They whistle a lot... get on your bloody nerves.
Hey man, I never said I was an ornithologist.

Communing with nature...
Well to tell yer the truth
I never actually got out the car,
But I could hear the wind and
see the clouds... er... scuddin...
Yeah that's about right... scuddin'
yeah that's about right!
Scuddin' moodily overhead.
Them black fluffy clouds really grim
lookin' don't know what they are
Hey do I look like a weatherman?

Anyway it was really something!
Like finding my roots,
Watching the petal-like wings of butterflies
er... pissing about,
Them white ones with black spots
Y'know the ones I mean?
They eat Tatie Leaves,
Fly about like they've been twatted.

I can't remember what they're called.
C'mon do I look like a Butterfly Collector?

Next time, I'm going native,
I'm getting out of the car,
I'm gonna touch trees, take time,
feel the earth rotate under my feet.
Y'know the one I mean?
Big blue thing, full of people
Dropping to bits, I forget its name!
Hey! do I look like an
Astronaut?

Just Another Beach Poem

The sea has been
told to stay behind
and writes endless
lines on an empty beach.

A seagull's wing
beaten by death,
fans sand across
lucky horseshoes.

The sun is still
the same busybodying
old schmuck,
head in clouds.
Cutting up rough
on pink podgy thighs.

Ice cream jerks off
onto bland pavement.

Punch and Judy,
with those new
social conscience
puppets,
the community worker
and the relate counsellor.

The sea acts out
its daily ritual,
Moons around
in wet dreams.

A coin in a slot
will buy you everything
but what you need.

Baz Lex Talio Nis

Bullied once too often
in the Juniors,
and dreading the
final bell.

On the long walk home
not daring to look back,
Leering voices scuffling
at my haversack straps.

Yells and commotion
cry-baby calls
mocking my misery.
and cowards yellow
making my guts ache.

Turning to face
my own fear,
and seeing Baz
dervishing his
towel bag into
the enemy ranks.
I charged and
we routed them
all.

Baz grinning
like a maniac,
at my muted appreciation
walked to my house
saluted and marched off.

Stopping only once
to empty the brick from his towelbag.

Baz and the Fascists

When Baz stopped bed wetting
and invited us up to the musty
fantasies of his secret passion,
It was like *Joplings'* window gone mad.
Mannequins kitted out with Nazi regalia,
a primitive arsenal of knives
and crossbows and rice-flails.
Like part of his childhood
got fucked up by the bastard brood
of Bruce Lee and Eva Braun.

One day pissed in Sunderland High Street,
Confronted by some National Front skin
with a copy of 'Bulldog' waving like a flag,
Baz took off his dut
and with rhino-like accuracy
Head-butted him to the ground,

and it was poppy day all over the place

'That's for me Grandad,' Baz muttered
moving off in search of new lethal weapons.

Baz Goes Dutch

Double
Dutch
in Holland.
Baz grasps
the fact
that his
vocabulary
does not extend
beyond its Northern
confines.
Gazes out of
the window
at Dutch swans
in Dutch canals
muttering.

'Look at all these
fuckin' fjords!'

Baz and the Ram Raiders

So anyway I'll tell yer
this is how it is,
We hot wired this Escort,
no rubbish mind we only Twoc G.T.s.
So anyway we took it to the town,
Ram raided the job centre
Not a fucking job on the premises
came out with half a dozen E.T. schemes
and some crap tapes of lift music.
Can't get rid of the E.T. schemes,
Sold the tapes to me Granny,
She's over the moon,
thinks it's James Last.

Got nicked last week
drivin' with no insurance,
no tax, no M.O.T….. no car,
Bastard surrealist coppers.

So anyway she sez
Yorra sexist pig, yer never take me anywhere,
Sez she's not gonna see me again unless I change…
Bought some Reeboks and
a new pair of Levis
Can't say I haven't tried.

Tell yer what to do
to stop them petrol bombs,
put the price of petrol up,
didn't see half the violence,
durin' the Gulf War.

How man you've never seen nowt like it,
it was bliddy great man
hundreds, na thousands of us
rampaging through the city,
Pouring over the Tyne Bridge,

It was like a revolution man.
I, a do the Great North run
every year.
Why it keeps us off the streets.

Between Rivers

Between rivers flows isolation.

Early bird takes flight over Worm Hill.
Barbed wire glinting in cowflesh.
Grey river alive with metal fish.
Driftwood is caught in the tree roots.
Between rivers

Turning the great eye downward
a merlin gutting mice.
In the tall stems of rape
harvesting women.

Bunting in Briggflatts
Eliot in Death's dream kingdom
Ferlinghetti remembering Ezra Pound.

Between rivers of words
silent as soil,
mossy as druid stone,
beneath
pinholes of light
congregate

stars…
perhaps
or reminders of stars.

Rising on thermals
early autumn leaves
blow into the dead
face of the city.

David Cormack Used to Tell

david cormack used to tell
us stories about his sister
until we grew clothes pegs
in our khaki shorts
I used to dream about her
but never found out
what to do with
clothes pegs until
later and by then
david cormack's sister
used to buy nappies
at the co-op.

Stealing Flowers Off

stealing flowers off
graves for mother's day
and cigarettes from
the paper shop was not
the same thing
mam always liked the
flowers
but we didn't
always like the
cigarettes.

When Barry Venners

when barry venners
stole my bike
he was kind
enough to
give me a ride
home first
so i was sad
to hear that he'd
got killed
under a bus
and told his dad so
when he
brought my bike
back.

The Worst Thing About

the worst thing about
being a little boy
is that no one listens
to you except other little
boys who don't bother to pick
you when it comes to football.
and little girls who say
they like you one minute
and the next minute
they run off to Singapore
cos their dad's in the army
and never give you back
the comics you lent them
and grow up into strangers
on buses when you haven't
had a wash and want to talk
to them and
god not listening
and P.E. teachers
and liking liquorice root.

Charlie Cole's Mausoleum

Called it a church
but god knows why,
twenty scruffy kids
in hand me down
faith.

Even had a choir
and an organ master
called Gabriel,
who we reckoned
had wings under
his off white
surplice.

Had lots of brass
but not a lot of class
had lots of candles
but not a lot of light.
Had lots of prayers
but not a lot of answers
had lots of singing
but not a lot of joy.

Called it a church
it cost two pence
on the bus,
it was then that
I lost my earthy soul.

Asked the reverend what made god,
but he only told me god didn't make me.

Chrissnings

Elbowed me to
the kerbside,
did me Father.
I elbowed him
back and got back to the path.
Shoved me like
a ha'penny
'cross the grey
flags, I shoved
him back and
nivver stood
on a crack.

Chrissning party
gave me brother
two shiny florins
and some chrissmus
cake cos they'd had
a girl.

Slapped me across
the heed,
did me father
called
me a daft bugger.
I took a stick
and chucked
it in the sky.

Uncle Kevin's Aquarium

We have won these goldfish annually
at hometown carnivals instead of cheap toys.
We have arrived at the number five
when all the other prizes are long dead;
smudges in jotters,
one sentence in the essay entitled
'What I did during half-term'.
I tell my children
not to bring goldfish home
but the irony of my pleas
has them hooked.
I am easy prey.
A small recompense
for the trawled oceans
I reason, considering this
cuboid of water.
We watch them swim
Give them slave names,
keep the water from stagnating
with pipes and pumps and electricity.
They are a burden on our economy.
They are a metaphor for guilt.
Swimming effortlessly
under a wooden sky
that holds up five
kitchen size matchboxes.

The Dynamo Field

A thousand footballs ago
down the scabby-kneed,
short back and sides of childhood.
We chalked stumps on a wall
and argued over dust.
Light failed us in the four-leaf clover
night of lucky innocence and stories
spun under arcing streetlights
pedalled our frightened bicycles
through the Frankenstein streets
with werewolves and vampires
at out bristling necks.
When blazing brambles sparked holes
in knitted pullovers until we reeked
of mackerel in the haystack torching
infernos on the dynamo field.

And oh! How we loved you then;
Mam and Dad in the fireside,
hot water bottle, candy stripe pyjama,
Channel eight and verichrome years.
With your arms about us,
And the double thickness of home
blanketing nightmare.

Waiting for Christmas trees
by frozen windows.

Pugilism

Got some boxing gloves one Christmas
and a punch ball, red leather, knocked hell out of it,
it never hit back.
Me and Kenny, one afternoon
had a boxing match
same Christmas present, see.
we sparred and lightly tapped each other,
he jabbed me once or twice, nicked my cheek
with rough sewn seams.
We floated like butterflies for a bit
and then he stung me like a bee
and opened up a lightning gash
under my left eye, with a hammered
home fist full of force and followed up
with a lethal combination
that left my nose spread
across my face all blood and snot.
I went fuckin' light
and pummelled him
with outrageous roundhouses
with him saying sorry and
putting his guard up to fend me off.
A sort of cross between
Raging bull and Tommy Steele's
Little White Bull.
I flailed until he pinned
me with a left hook
that put me down
and counting backwards
in frustration.

I swapped my gloves for a subbuteo.

Kenny got put in Borstal for knifing his Dad.

Remembering Norman

I was remembering Norman.
Never any good at football,
His hands fidgeting down the front
of his unfashionable football shorts.
Open season for every would-be bully.

At the school gates at home time,
Beaten once again in an unfair fight,
You cried; before, during and after blows;
And I knew then that those were not the
First to go astray.

Later, caught trying to steal affection
From your Mam's purse,
You bought sweets, to buy friends
Who lasted as long as a penny chew.

And your Dad,
Big Anglican, little man
With your frightened Mother,
Kneeling at the altar on Sunday mornings.
Pious, Christian bully boy,
Beating little boys like you
and your brother.
Red handed in the urine soaked sheets,
He beat you,
So you wet the bed,
And your father beat you
for wetting the bed.

In the musty air of your bedroom.
You told me simply,
'Sometimes I wet the bed'
And I did not have the courage
Or the understanding
to tell you that, it didn't matter.

Norman. It didn't matter.

Too late, as it happens.

This powerless apology.

Meadow Avenue, 1963

We had a cemetery
outside of the house
where I lived as a kid.

Mam said it was full
of people who had died
and gone to Heaven
which seemed to
be a contradiction.

Dad said that Grandad
was sleeping there now,
which was what he used
to do when he was alive
only in an armchair and
smoking a pipe.

You should never sing in
 a graveyard I was told,
because if you do all
of the people in it will
haunt you for being happy.
At Sunday school
the vicar used to sing
even when he was talking
this made me miserable.
I always used to wear
my best frown when I
put flowers where
Grandad slept
this made Mam
happy although
she liked blowing
her nose a lot.

At night you could
hear people shouting

and closing their gates
and smell stale beer
and cigarettes.

Toffee Apples and Smoked Fish

At the Football match
Dad would drink coffee
out of his thermos flask,
Laced with whiskey to
keep us warm, I'd learn
new swear words and
ponder the lineage of
referees.
afterwards
we would walk
to the market;
all fish and toffee apples,
all smoke and racket,
all lard and dripping,
and
I would hold his hand
although I was too big,
as I would today
if he were here.

Poetry United

What d'yer call that Normal man, you've got to be more
alert than that man, I know you've been concentratin' on
telly lately but the season's nearly over kidda, Poetry's the
name of the game, Howay man, Zepheniah play the ball
give it to Hegley something of a comedian aren't yer.
Armitage! you're holdin' on to the ball for far too long
man, get the bloody thing movin' give it some wellie, get
it to Cleary, the Ryan Giggs of poetry this boy.
Knock it out to the left wing, Gan on Yevgeny!
Ferfucksake Harrison where's your fuckin head at were
you on the pop last night or what?
Christ on a kebab! Duffy man, howay lass, get the ball
pushed up through the middles. Give it to McGough.
Not like that!
Mitchell! Keep yer eye on the ball... Go on my son!
Do I not like that! Do I not like that!
Shit! Offside! that was never offside!
Ref! Foul! Man Foul!
That was a friggin' penalty, that Ref's blind!
Dirty player that Cadwallender.
I'm takin' Heaney off.

Gardeners' Question Time

i could write about the flowers that grow in your garden
and look up all the latin names I could spout out polemic
and quote the manifesto and spell exactly Lenin's middle name
i could take you to the wine bar and apologise for having no money
i could say i'm sorry you think Tony Blair wandered into my study
i could shout about revolution and the need for change but you'd
just think me foolish when really i'm deranged. because I can
appreciate your poetry with its implicit political agenda but when
i use mine to protest you just think i'm on a bender. i could write
about the flowers that grow in your garden, but i'd use them as a
metaphor for the north-south divide, because my life isn't full of
conservatories and patios and the only type of barbecue i like is
the one that Guido tried. so excuse me for swearing and spoiling
your coffee morning, excuse me for breathing the same air as you.
i could write about the flowers that grow wild in my garden but
i'll never understand what it's got to do with you.

Love on a Branch Line

on the metro, rab says he's in love with
the woman who says, 'Mind the doors, Please'
i tell him it's a machine but he's smitten anyway.
as he leaves the train he knows he'll maybe never
hear that voice again, he knows he'll always
'Mind the doors' cos she's stuck in his head
like the lord's prayer, like the ten times table
like an ice pick.
we board another train but the voice is a man
a man who doesn't ken rab, who rab doesn't love
and he pines for her gentle reassurance and certainty.
but she's unfaithful and like an answerphone
hopelessly attentive to duty. she is breaking poets
hearts up and down the east coast line. with a
poet in every terminus and her limited vocabulary.
rab says the Tyne bridge is beautiful at sunrise and i
can see regret, pulling the emergency cord,
inverting timetables, returned ticketing him
back to Newcastle in winter, when she'll be there
consistent if repetitious, and finding her at last
re-enacting ' strangers on a train '.
pulling in to Glasgow central julie says
there must be a woman somewhere that made
that recording. but there's no romance in that,
there's no romance in the attainable, it's only
when you think it can never happen, that it happens.
and rab's love is pure. it is not tainted by flesh,
he is not enthralled by just lust; this is spiritual,
this is disembodied, like a poem outside of a poet,
like the speaking clock, it's nothing personal,
it's nothing rational.
julie, is finishing her white wine and slipping
between tired sheets.
rab has a voice in his head like the clear white light
and soon he'll be calling out her name
and talking in tongues.

Home Defense

Overtaken by paranoia and
the vital need for what the Americans call
'Home Defense'.
I am looking for somewhere to hide
the machete I've just bought from a local
butcher-it-yourself shop.
I find some gaffa tape and
hoist it up snugly under my desk,
testing it out for accessibility,
for ease of swing against some unexpected,
unsuspected intruder.
I keep it honed to perfection.
It slips as easily as a knife through some nutter.
No one will violate my possessions.
Later in bed I contemplate 'hand-to-hand' combat
between myself and a burglar who has discovered
my secret machete… I lose.
I creep cautiously downstairs and exchange
the machete for a Swiss army knife I keep in my pyjamas,
and later pondering the wisdom of my actions
bring all three weapons to bed.
I contemplate throughout the staircase creaking night,
the options available to me;
Karate courses, Rottweillers,
Burglar alarms, Electric Fences.

I am frightened of the burglar who might have a gun.
I am frightened of the burglar with the psycho friend who
is only made angry by machetes.

I am afraid for my wife and children,
I consider the purchase of automatic weapons for her
and maybe Derringers for the kids.
my wife has sleepless nights
due to my insomnia

She says I should try to close my eyes and rest.

She is frightened for me or maybe of me.
The machete winks in the moonlight.
Maybe I'll buy a shotgun.

In the cold crisp common sense morning,
I unilaterally disarm, stockpile my weapons
for disposal, Telephone freephone insurance.

During the night my car has been stolen.

Baz Ich Bin Ein Berliner

'Look at the state of that wall!
It'll take a good brickie to put that lot right.'

Baz Erotica

Derek sez,
He's got this mate,
Works in a dirty book factory.
Can get yer anything yer like,
Swedish, soft porn,
Hard core, S & M,
Animals, Bondage,
Someone's Granny,
Readers' Wives,
Anything yer fancy!
Cheap as well.

Baz turns his nose up, mutters into his pint,
'Fuck that, I'd rather have a wank!'

The Building Trade

Julian is an existentialist. He works on a building site
with Tom the labourer, Fred the brickie and Bob the hod carrier.
It works like this: Tom fills Bob's hod up with bricks,
Bob carries them to Fred and Fred builds a wall.
Julian's job is to help the bricks understand their own reality.

Tom has ham sandwiches for lunch, Bob has cheese and Fred has egg.
Julian doesn't have lunch as he feels this is saying 'no'
to a society which insists on social imperatives such as lunch.

Sometimes the bricks argue with Julian saying
'But we have the right to freedom'
Julian smiles, 'man is condemned to freedom'
'But we are bricks' they cry, 'why do you oppress us?'
Some days the walls just don't get built at all.
Julian doesn't sleep well.
He dreams of a mass uprising of bricks,
of boundaries collapsing all over suburbia,
of Sunday morning street warfare with flymos
and hovers clashing over disputed inches of turf,
of middle-class landowners with nothing to keep
their mortgages in…
Secretly,
Tom practises hod carrying
Bob practises bricklaying
and Fred is doing a night class in sociology.
Julian is an existentialist and lives outside
of the restrictions placed upon him by the
constant problem of having no self to esteem
and no self to be 'ish' with
this however does not prevent his sleeping
with the gaffer's daughter who has
a Btec in Freudian hairdressing,
which means that every time
she cuts someone's hair
they look like a dick.

Callous in Sunderland

Walking the Chester Road
with you shouting maliciously
'You arrogant bastard!'
made me feel as if I was
about to be written out
of a soap opera
and
when you slapped my face,
I was surprised how much
it didn't hurt and that the
sound created was not quite
in synch.
and might have to be dubbed
later.
I mouthed my scripted apology;
you played Greta Garbo and
melodrama.
I opted for bathos;
our ratings went through the roof.

god, how you would have laughed,
opening this letter from a passer-by
who imagines we are real.

Much later we made love,
although I was using a
stunt double for the tricky orgasmic bit.

Unsolved Mysteries

There are some things no man can comprehend.
Lurking in the skirting board of the subconscious mind.
Hiding like a discarded chip on the floor behind the cooker.
Whimpering like a puppy in the cold and heartless kennel.

Unsolved mysteries. Supernatural phenomena.
Tales from beyond belief. Spooky Things!

In the first of our startling new series;
James Dean: Legendary star of *Giant*,
East of Eden
And *Rebel without a Cause*.
We ask the question,
'Was he a rubbish driver or what?'

Jackie Onasis. World famous for marrying the rich and
powerful
We ask the question never before asked from the grassy
knoll of television
'Why did, she try and catch all those bits of brains and
head?'

Mystic Meg: Lottery Clairvoyant and sad old slapper journalist.
Why don't you crawl back under the Russell Grant rock of tacky
astrology?

Unsolved mysteries. Supernatural phenomena.
Tales from beyond belief. Spooky Things!

O. J. Simpson. Actor, Ex Proball star and very slow van driver.
Why do you buy gloves that are two sizes too small?

Uri Geller: Psychic and Sales Rep for Sheffield Stainless
Steel Cutlery.
we ask the question on the lips of couch potatoes everywhere.
If you're so clairvoyant what's me Mam called?

Michael Portillo ex-member of parliament,
ex-golden boy of politics,
ex-next prime minister of Torytown.
Do the words eat shit mean anything to you?

Unsolved mysteries. Supernatural phenomena.
Tales from beyond our House. Spooky Things!

Steven

steve, not being one for violence
went down under the weight of their words.
Bugger,
Queer,
Bastard Ponce.
ricochets of leather on skin, boots on footballs
and all the pent up rage of boys struggling to
define their manhood.

steve, not being one for violence
held his head, lay back and thought of
england kicking the shit out of him.
and over a few pints they rejoiced
at their victory, staggered to dole queues
with pride hard in their pants.

steve, not being one for violence
understood,
'that's the way it is'
he grinned,
'rather me than someone else'

It was then that I realised.
he was more of a man then
I could ever be.

True Colours

Tracy has two babies; one black, one white,
she calls them her own private Toon army.
takes them to sit in the stands.
one of them was once kissed by Kevin Keegan
on a day when the press were invited.
Tracy spends her benefit on season tickets
and babygros. breast feeds behind the
opposition goal, has a tattoo on her wrist
of a magpie, collects autographs like silver paper,
precious little names glued on the walls of her nest.
waiting for the landlord to come and fix the gas fire.
decided her kids would be better off in the care
of rugby union supporters. Left a scribbled note;
black biro on white and two kids wrapped in a
hand-knitted scarf in away colours.

Urban Muse

If I had to have a muse I would call her Susan.
Rising from dishwater and the fumes from her car exhaust.
She would dance on Fridays and be interested in cosmetics.
she would drink pints to excess and carry the arsenal
of poetry in a patent leather handbag.
She would teeter on stilettos
to the nightclubs, hiding bottles of gin
in her coat and turn bouncers into poets.
She would have one blind eye to ignore
my failings and an unbelievable, unreasonable
faith in my poetic powers.
She would be made out of concrete and tobacco
and do her shopping in Aldi,
I would call her up at all hours of the night
and say get round here I feel a poem coming on.
She would be wise and mysterious
and tell me 'to get a grip'
or a life, or a day job.
I would worship her
at the shrine of her independence,
She would reject my emotions recollected in tranquillity,
For a scribbled note on the back of a betting slip
written between the off licence and an
empty bottle of vodka.
She would be working class
and scoff at my middle class pretensions,
I would call her Susan
and she would call me behind my back
but her answerphone would
always listen to my late night depressions
when she was not available
and take me out for curries
and tell me when Susan
had deserted me for a romantic poet.

Moscow Cowboys

gunfight at the Boris Yeltsin corral.
red stars and Sigue Sigue sputnik.
she's line-dancing in Lenin's tomb,
drinking like a Cossack
at a Macdonald's drive-thru.

and all the Moscow cowboys
are drinking Budweiser
posing in Levis
and swapping
soviet brown bear hats
for Stetsons.

The Bolshevik Edge

Mayakovsky got it right,
put a bullet in it
before it got out of control
and between
blood and women,
chose blood.

In the Rosta windows
drawing workers with
his eyes closed,
swollen fingers
muffled against the cold.

'We don't need a dead temple of art
where dead workers languish, but a
living factory of the human spirit'

The hammer bends the sickle
the wheels that forged motion
grind to memoirs of revolution.
Mayakovsky got it right,
After all this time.

Buying chic Bolshevism
from galleries, the
blood of Mayakovsky
on a thousand different
walls.

The Beekeeper's Son

Honey-fingered
David entertains
a swarming hand
stung by innocence,
A little boy with
a scrum of bees.

Children, mouths ajar
in the puns of summer.
Dandelion heads and
jam-red lips.
Busy as bodies
in the killing glass.
Pollen counting
up to ten.
The adult net catches
all comers.

.....and someone made them all,
and someone great or small,
if not God, then someone
half-wise or merely wonderful,
had a moment of blinding alacrity,
Got their fingers in the meld
of tiny wings.

The Tempest

for Desmond Graham

Caliban Edwards the worse for twenty years of drink
really believes that this barmaid who has heard it all
before is the one for him. Lurches up and orders one
for the road, gabbles out some perfunctory remark
before slipping out to the take away and the usual
clammy hand under the duvet.
and love is a forlorn hope
in this grubby little world
and why bother with romance
when you don't know the steps
to this erroneous dance.
Miranda Richards clears away the debris
catches a taxi to her mother's ideal home,
lies awake thinking of all the flotsam that
floats on the head of a gallon of drink. tells herself
that amongst the drips who gather around the drip
trays there must be one who is special.
Closes her eyes
thinks about a jacket in Dorothy Perkins' window.
and love is a mystery to itself
it is unable to contemplate how
low it has fallen and like every
precious commodity depreciates
in the passing of days.
Ferdinand Jenkins has a fax and a mobile phone
writes love letters to strangers on the internet,
books a bucket seat for a desperate fortnight
on some god forsaken island.

Baz and the Freedom of the Press

Full of Hell, Baz gatecrashes the chip shop,
bringing down on the counter a greasy
newspaper, bearing a colour image
of a topless model.

'It's a fucking disgrace, you should
watch what you're selling,
I bought them chips for my little girl'

The chip shop owner is
caught somewhere between
bemused and terrified and
pours two lots of vinegar
over some wifie's tail-end.

He stutters meekly.
'But… I only sell chips.'

Baz explodes,
'Bloody typical!
I bet you're a Tory.
Only a bloody Tory rag
would print this filth
and only a Tory would
wrap up a little girl's chips
in pornography.'

The chip shop queue
are nodding their agreement
and checking their wrappings for nudes.

'But… but.. I'm only doing my job.'
'Oh yeah, I've heard that excuse before
from a guard in Auschwitz as I remember!'

The poor bastard is sweating now
and apologizing, he offers Baz
a free fish and chip lunch.

Baz graciously accepts the offer
The queue warmly applauds
his morality and his heroic exit.

Outside I remind Baz
that he hasn't got a little girl,
he reminds me
who's got the free lunch.

Anarchy in the UK

Swapping your bondage trousers
for the articles of a law you could not endorse,
was not the brightest spanner
you ever threw into the works.
Now we sit in silence.
You tell me to watch your coat
as you go for a slash.
'Someone might steal it'
you inform me.
I dredge a memory from the back catalogue
of your convictions.
and
think you are right
Someone might.
Ten years ago it might have been you.

Islam, Bagels and Geronimo's Cadillac

I walked for three blocks in search of cigarettes,
Saturday afternoon, March, Brooklyn, in the Jewish quarter,
Not one human being anywhere and not a single sound,
Watching grey squirrels foraging at the kerbside,
I bought a pack of Marlborough from a kiosk on 14th Avenue.

In a moment of bizarre solitude and alienation
I whistled a Gerard Kenny song and decided that
it didn't get any better wherever you whistled it.

I walked the three blocks back to the rooms above the bagel shop
where my relatives lived, chain smoking and wondering if
I should walk like a stranger or a native.

when the world finally stubs itself out
this is what it will look like I told myself.

Koli had made food, rice and okra curry,
Kanchan spoke about Atlantic City.
Shabnam smiled at me as I ate with my fingers,
I think I was as happy as I have ever been.

Percy Shelley's Lungs

Geordie says he knows how Shelley felt
when the water entered his lungs.
Ten years of Emphysema have seen to that
and when he was younger and fitter
he could have supped absinthe until
Coleridge and all his devils had passed out
and Byron's clubfoot was nothing
compared to the injury that invalided
him out of the army and into the pits
and Wordsworth, well at least he had
his health and could go on nice long walks
and Blake was barking mad and saw
ghosts of fleas which were nothing compared
to what Geordie had seen in Singapore,
Christ, man, I could be a romantic poet,
easy, just give me the fucking chance!
Just give me the fucking chance!

The Paint Lasts Longer than the Skin

I met him once in Peterlee Labour Club
all tuxedo and cigar and brylcreemed hair,
He was drinking from a short glass with ice
and he smiled at me as though I wasn't there.

Some say that Andy Capp was based on little Bobby,
and Dennis the Menace's jumper
owed something to the man
and that characteristic woodbine
at a certain obscure angle
well who's to say where Humphrey Bogart got it from?
and that surge of interest in the seventies –
the album, the tour, the fresh acclaim,
Bobby they reckon was sharp as Max Miller
and Charlie Chaplin was almost the same.
and Buster Keaton looked uncannily like him
and in a certain light Big John Wayne.
If truth be told he was the Second Coming
Slouching towards Penshaw to be born

In the Casino Royale late in a life
a far cry from the short red pens
and rich men's horses,
Gambling on a reputation
and the swell in an audience's hearts.

When I think of him on and off stage
I think of two separate men.
When I think of him I wonder where
the man ends and the comic begins,
They say that illusion comes from the inside
and that the paint lasts longer than the skin.

Get Billy Elliot

Easington, I love you more than all
The strafed holes in the walls of the Trust,
Easington you are a hard and gentle community,
drinking my cup of tea opposite
the boarded eyes of the 'Black Diamond',
listening to researchers on their mobiles
talking about people as if they were
a different species.
Easington I have read my poems to you,
in the listed buildings in the village
and alongside Mary Nightingale Bell
in the club opposite where the pit
used to spin reflected in the wheels of these
Christmas bikes slightly rusty in October.
Playing pool in the Rafa
under the polystyrene wings
of spitfires and hurricanes shot
to pieces by generations of vandals
and now Billy Elliot pirouettes
through your 'back to backs' like
nothing much has changed since the war,
when everything has changed.
Gutted by successive governments
like the fish in the soup kitchens
and
like me, in tears at the
rows of donated toys for children.
I could mention Heather Wood,
I could mention Ken Bell,
I could mention Paul Getty II,
I could mention Davey Hopper,
I could mention Paul Wilkinson,
I could mention King Arthur,
I could mention the 'American butcher'.
History will record its own version of events.
'Ghost villages, epitaphs to lost
opportunites' as someone once wrote,

not meaning quite that.
Billy Elliot slips on his tights
in a southern stereotype that it's only
'grim up north' and that art is
a foreign concept to its quaint
'poor' folk who know all there is
to know about whippets and ferrets
but beyond that fall short by a brow.
'London,
you're a big city
but you're out of condition!'

Train in Norris Minor

We've had leaves and cows and the
wrong kind of snow,
that delay us going anywhere let
alone where we want to go,
We've had derailment, denouements
and denationalisation,
Trains out of fuel with terse
announcements at each station.
We've had floods and power cuts
and vandalism to blame,
We've had resignations and
restrictions and now there's a new
game.

It's called putting up with anything
it's the truly British way
It's a test for our stiffer upper lips as
each criticism comes our way,
In the case of an emergency an
accountant will arrive
and restore public confidence as
stock and shares take a dive.
And in case that isn't enough for us
dreadful human beings
Who slog it out on commuter trains
and watch the dirty dealings
of second hand car salesmen who
slum it in their limousines,
One man's reputation is the state of
the job they're leaving.

You can put your trust in
governments practised in pulling the wool
or be content with the political
commentators adept at shovelling bull,
You can kid yourself democracy
is alive and shacked up with

freedom of choice,
But as a drunken poet once said
and he was right, 'Shout revolution
and you'll lose your voice!'

Red Trevor

I have bought books from him before
and fish.
His carrier bag is legendary in the bar.
the last book he sold me
was
Field, Factories and Workshops Tomorrow
by Peter Kropotkin.
Trevor says
the end is good
but the theory is dodgy.

I ask for kippers
he talks about
his dogma
as if it means something.

I am only interested in hunger.
he talks about 'mutual aid'
and inventive genius.

I buy us both a drink.
We watch the same football match
on the same television,
His side is losing.
He will not admit it.

He promises me fish
next week and more books
many more books.

Chez Guevara

slumped in front of the tv
riddled with the bulletins
from the latest armed coup.
Wondering if that razor blade
in the bathroom is sharp enough
for one last close shave.

Khaki underwear drying,
faded camouflage for
the play station photo shoot.
a walk on role in Evita
in the west end and then
a poster in the Athena
end of season sale.

feeling less than legendary.
eyes full of bluebottle larvae.

Someone, somewhere
has disconnected the
revolution.

Ten Problematical Things to Say to a Woman Bus Driver on Boarding the Sunderland Bus

with apologies to Adrian Mitchell for stealing his wheelbarrow

1. Patronising
If you need any help on the big corners
just give me a shout and I'll be please to do it for you, pet.

2. Sexist
What's a pretty girl like you doing driving on a big bus like this.
It's a shame that they did away with bus conductresses.

3. Lecherously
I like a woman who can handle big loads.

4. Misguided Politically Correct
You have a perfect right to drive this bus.
I shall enjoy this as much, if not more
than a similar journey with a driver
of the opposing gender.

5. Homophobically
There's no reason why a lesbian such as
yourself can't do the job as well
as a 'normal' person.

6. Metaphysically
Mighty are the bus stops of the soul
and you are the Amazonian charioteer
of Time's winded chariot.

7. Informatively
During wartime many women drove buses
and indeed ambulances and other public utility vehicles.
Ultimately leading to a post-war discontent amongst
women as a work force. Historically this has proved

to be of lasting consequence and a positive factor
in the battle for equality and emancipation.
Oh and do you stop outside of Asda?

8. Mysogynsitically
Carry on madam. I shall wait for the
next conveyance which has a man at the wheel.

9. Marxist
This red bus is a metaphor for the unending class struggle
and this exchange of money between myself and yourself
will inevitably lead to the fall of the bourgeoisie capitalist
state and thus the creation of a new world order!

10. Liberal Apologetically
I have nothing against women drivers.
Don't get me wrong, some of my best friends are women.

However, in my experience
the best thing to say upon a bus driven by a
woman
is; £3.20 return to Sunderland, please.

Sundland

for Alistair Robinson

Alice, what's the matter?
Is the Stadium of light too bright
For your Victoriana eyes?
At home at the secret door in Mowbray Park,
Where words now bloom on benches
And Crawford nails his replica shirt to the mast.
In this new boiled city with its football shaped heart
And that luminous eye blinking in and out of the river
Under the span of Burdon's bridge and its
Mythical silver rivet.
Drink this brown river and grow.

Gull City
5 a.m.
Rich pickings from
Last night's beer babies.
Tearing into fast food cartons
Pizza beaked
Kentucky fried albatross.

Today the news reported seagulls dropping like flies
An inappropriate simile
Seagulls dropping like litter.
The council road sweeper
Slices through a broadside of wings
Like a trawler.

The capillaries of trees mesh the morning
The tight weave of nests capturing feathers
As light cracks the white of sky with yolk.
Whistling now their shrill blue symphony
The birds have forgotten the words.

High on Tunstall Hill
In collective nouns and plurals,

Gathering their sentences to speak,
The crows like rorschachs are
Open to interpretation.

In Turner-esque half-light
Cross-hatched shadows stretch their lines
To reel in darkness from the night,
Abandoned melody of moon, opening
Onto overtures of cold silver spilling
Over the leeward side of sleep
And the sleepers.

Scrambling for cover
Motorbikes and butterflies
Dead for Winter.
Both will return.
Technicolor inkblots
Settling for warmth
And pause
On scorched earth
Left by twockers.

And in the nooks and crevices
Snails cranny .
Their Autumn shells in clusters
Like grapeshot echoing the cannonball limestone.

Claire explains technicalities
While her mobile gives out
And yellow wort pushes up between her boots.
I am cast as the naturalist's apprentice

Guessing games of hawthorn and elderberry,
The heart-shaped sorrel seeds on my sleeve,
Rain looming overhead and smouldering ash,
Spitting spitefully from some ruined car.

'I know whose car that is!' says one of the Bash Street Kids,
Dragging his trainers through this 'important geological site'
Schooldays or not, bravado to the fore,

'It's a bloke what wants the insurance!'

We leave the sight
Talking about Dingy skippers
And Painted Ladies as if the words were romance
Rather than sticks carried by blotched petals
Returning from 'the Med'
To unpredictable thistled quarries.

Alice, what's the matter?
Under Ozymandian viaducts
Beside the Queen Alexander Bridge
Or watching rust bud on metal trees
Near stone books and bicycles framed
On gateways to history.
Replacing ships and
The heavy dray horses thundering
Down streets like a Vaux beer barrel
Into the cellar at 'The Brewery Tap'

Alice
Did you fall asleep and wake up out of work?
Eat this and try not to forget.

Sunderland Ascendant

for Peter Camm

Before I open my eyes
This dream of rising and setting.
Of coal blackened bricks
And red and white hands
Under low slung roofs at Wearmouth Colliery.
Like embers of memory,
Industry phoenixed by leisure.

'In Sunderland did Peter Reid
 a stately pleasure dome decree
Where Wear the sacred river ran
Through shipyards measureless to man
Down to a shipless sea.'

The Stadium of light from darkness
Piggy backed on the bowed legs of a monument,
Fire from coal,
Shipwrecked on the banks of the Wear
The white ribs of some ancient titanic animal,
Lowing in the floodlit evenings.

St.Peter's for sanctuary
Take a handful of tablets and lie down forever.

The cursed family, the cauld lad, the horned moses,
The Masonic heraldry, the snake temple on Penshaw hill,
The ancient and the ruined, Spirits and shuggy boats,
The ghost of Lewis Carroll passes through the council van
That maintains a castle on the brink, the council workman
Lights a cigarette, smoke creeps up the blighted sandstone
To the figures petrified on time stormed battlements.

The gates to nowhere, the buried exits or entrances,
Fallen arches and word games, my aching feet.

Phoenix lodge has windows of obsidian glass
And where the local disaffected non- Masonic rituals
Of youth have smashed away the veneer
Paranoia and masonry, bricks and mortar,
Concealing hidden treasure and Sunderland's
Aproned past.
…and yes it looks better than this now,
the set square and compass revitalised,
doors flung open in invitation
a bird lays its eggs in fire
in the mystical east… end.
A blindfolded man could throw a stone
In the direction of Holy trinity,
Out of work now, claiming redundancy,
Guardian of Crawford's bones.
Where the kids play football when they
Can get away with it and the shades of
Burke and Hare whisper secrets.

The curfew tolls the knell of parting day,
The seagulls cry in from the coldest blue,
School children homeward plod their weary way
And leave the world to darkness and to you.

Prior's vision in magnesium limestone set ,
Solemn, splendour, a pre-Raphaelite house
Legends of art and craft in every transept
Gill and Morris and Wells to Thompson's mouse.

For thee, who mindful of the honoured dead,
Dost in thy lines their artful tales relate,
I stand in awe by lonely contemplation led,
At the 'Adoration of the Magi' or beneath the Lych gate.

I mourn and praise you at the stained glass beasts
By the Lady chapel and the egg-tempera seas
By Bucknall's burnished iron cross and Macdonald's Eve,
I mourn and praise the treasure of artists such as these.

Andrew was a fisherman who knew the net and reel,
In this shipwrecked cathedral, this upturned keel,
We are cast adrift souls under a buttressed dome,
Flooded by light and colour, sailing to kingdom come,

Large was their bounty and their souls sincere
Heaven's art a recompense for all who visit here,
In the quiet lawns at Roker, famed for other roars,
The beauty of the craftsman's art behind these heavy doors.

St. George's blushing nationwide league brickwork,
Red and black like staithes,
A grim church spawned by the bombed out Victoria Hall,
What would £2000 get you these days
A P-reg Corsa from Bristol Street Motors.

Square set Mountain Daisy, holding out against new elements,
Snug tiles in mock baroque fashion leaned against by drinking men
'To spare thee now is past my power, thou bonnie gem.'
Burns said that although he too was 'on the square.'

Days of Empire, faded Terpsichore, sister of my own muse,
Gone the Palace, Gone the Kings, Gone the Avenue.

Sid James has just died in Sunderland.
Don't worry everybody dies in Sunderland.

A stone for Vesta Tilley and for Tommy Atkins and Piccadilly
          Johnny,
The echo of voices and laughter, good naturedly singing,
'For she's a jolly good fellow!'

Days of Empire, faded Terpsichore.

At the New Minster I am drinking coffee and crumpets
Under the gaze of memorial stones, Richardson and his relict,
A shipbuilder and his Missus. My dad worked on ships.
He has no place to mark where his body lies.

The oldest houses in the Sundered Land,

Beer and chips are apt if bland,
And although I would have preferred a
More fitting tribute or
Even an apostrophe before the other 'place'
A pun the journalists at the Echo might embrace.

And the glory of the waterworks is somehow blurred
By speeding authority vans and hefty bills incurred,
By phallic chimneys that have given up smoking
To become works of art, you must be joking.
Beauty is in the things that we endeavour
To keep in their present state forever.

The home of Lord and Lady water
Horded in pools there deep blue treasure.

Look yonder, Sancho
There is only one outrageous giant!
I think I can take him if you hold my pint.
The red and white river flows down North Bridge Street
From the Flailing mill returning to the source of light.
Light from the Railway King's Monkwearmouth station,
Light from the Davey Lamp outside the ground,
Light from the old south pier lighthouse
Beached at Cliff Park.

Doxford where the engineers came to dream of metal
And sailed their bolted hulls out seaward and spawned
Bright yesterdays and bitter loss.

Where once the gentlefolk mused in terraced splendour
Homes for Kings then, Now only music vendors,
Foyle Street and John Street with history to let,
These iron clad houses fallen shibboleths.

And
Street after street and street and blushing red magnificence,
Mean, moody and municipal.

At Mackie's corner where lovers once would meet,
Woo'd by starry eyes and a few pennorth of sweets,

To the refuge and the terraces, family homes and student
        retreats,
And this is where I live
And this is where I breathe
Between the stately decline and the deep blue sea,

They are cold inside and decoration takes forever,
They stand as memorials to Victorian stamina and endeavour
Row after row of rattling sashes against more than a century of
        bad weather
I think those Mackem Victorians must have had skin as tough
        as leather.
They tumble out of the past as if everyone was wealthy
Stumbling giant houses built for those with plenty.
Line upon line and window upon window
Columns and cornice, Shutters and shellac.

Build me a multiplex
It's a bright new word,
Flexible, plastic and mildly absurd,
Build me a multiplex
And take away death, marriage and birth
All three are old fashioned and all three can hurt.

Highs and lows, from grandeur to modest bungalows,
A home is a place with walls when the north wind blows,
Painted like wagons and arranged in neat rows,
Highs and lows, from grandiose to bungalows.

No ticky-tacky here, just pride and at last
A memorial to the 'not so great' who have passed.

Before I close my eyes
On the lofty and the low,
Before I close my eyes
And dream of what I know.

In the beginning God said
'Let there be light!'
And let it be red and white striped

And stand it in my sea that I might
Be reminded of the North East life
And make my planets move the fates
And poets and angels legislate
A Sunderland ascendant.

Baz Nativity

A virgin birth
on Boxing Day,
Christ knew where the father was.
Baz was born bloody
and cursed,

the umbilical cord
twisted about his neck,
blue with cold rage
and daring
God to take him …

if he were hard enough.

Magi backing away
not wanting any trouble.

Baz Inherits a Dad

When Baz's Mam got married
Baz got a Dad,
I remember his tears
burns cut his mucky cheeks,
the first time he was strapped.

He showed me the welts
of skin underneath his jumper,
I told him my sister had headlice
to cheer him up.

We went to point at her
as she wailed under her fine-tooth comb.

He said,
'It's great Kev,
I've never had a Dad
who beats you like a Dad should'

I lay awake thinking about those words
but couldn't grasp the logic.

My head itched through thinking too much.

Baz in the Perfumed Gardens

School sportsday
in the 1500 metres
Baz once stopped
to chat up a lass
from the Catholic School.
He came last
and got six
on each hand
but he reckoned
it was worth it.

Later and with
a lovebite *in situ*
he charged us 20 pence
to smell his middle finger.

Baz Karaoke

*'It means empty orchestra
but what does that mean?'*

Baz stretches the term vocal stylist to its limits

honking through a tearful *My Way*
and bastard filing the edges off *I will Survive*

dueting with Julie on *You're the One That I Want*,
a ghastly Travolta and a size 16 out of tune Sandy,
breathless in beer kissed moments

their kids hiding their faces
beneath hands suddenly too small.

'It means empty orchestra', Baz repeats
as if saying it twice will bring enlightenment.

Keeling over in the Labour club
like a diseased elm.

Baz Donne

In a world of air and angels
Baz at the end of his tether,
incapable of convalescence,
gasping at life and waiting
for the iron bishop to give
the last rites.
Bites back on the swirl
of the pipes that surround him
in a haze of ventolin he
reaches for his cigarettes.
Maybe he'll go out
in a blaze of glory,
blowing up the oxygen
taking some of these poor bastards
with him, but strength is failing
and his skin stretches over his bones
like gold to airy thinness
beaten and bowed, raises his eyes
to the clouds and skulking angels,
the last words of a devil,
whispered to
the prettiest nurse,

'Fucked ….

The Right Way to do Wrong

Be discreet, history will forgive
anything but bad manners,
Be charming, commit every act of treason
with grace and a winning smile.
Be astute, some may call this cunning.
Be noticed, be wrong and at all costs
be wrong in the most memorable way
possible.

I was wrong once or so I thought
it turns out I was mistaken.

Be affable, allow fools the room to rush
and angels to have their toes crushed in the push
and pull of the paradox.

Be laudable, keep your affairs politic,
Be found in the right bed by the right people
Never in the wrong bed by the wrong people.
Be infamous yet a diplomat,
A roué with style, a rogue with grace,

The right way to do wrong
changes as quickly as the ages,
Be consistent,
always commend the virtue
of what your other hand is doing
Be dependable, always know the name
of the person you are screwing.

The Wrong Way to do Right

Everything you say
From this point on
Will be held against you.
Don't mention love
It is too vague

Everything you do
From this day forth
Will be noted and used
In future arguments
Don't mention fidelity
It is archaic

Everything you know
From the first to now
Will be questioned closely
Challenged incessantly
Brutalised endlessly
Don't mention hope
It does not want to exist
Don't mention honour
It is obsolete

The wrong way to do right
Is as misguided
As the right way to do wrong.

Aaaargh!

In the beginning was the word
Unfortunately the word was aaaargh
AAARGH it said
Look at all this darkness and floaty bits
AAARGH it said
Look at all this water it is too wet
AAARGH
Look at all these fishies crawling out of the water
AAARGH
That's evolution that.
AAARGH
Look at all this void, what's the point of void, it's well…void.
Strictly Speaking , said a cliché, *You are not a proper word!*
AAARGH said the AAARGH
I am not a proper word
Well you're not in my dictionary
AAARGH said the AAARGH
I am not in the dictionary, then
He paused,
What is a dictionary?
Ignorance is bliss, said the cliché.
Humppffh said AAARGH
Who was being deliberately onomatopoeic
AAARGH said the cliché not to be outdone by a non word.
In the beginning was the word
And the word was God
Said a noun ,
That's not a word said AAARGH
You're just making that up.
And he floated off looking for adjectives
To describe himself.

Colouring in Guernica

Take out your books and brains
You are going to experience art
whether you want to or not.
Well it's bit dull but it's only
a photograph of a painting.
And a black and white one at that,
I bet the colours are spectacular like Gaudi
Yes, Gaudi's the one whose buildings
look like melted candles in the Tapas bar
on Gray Street, He was Italian or Spanish and
dead I think. Was that a cathedral?
I thought it was a painting!
What's it called? funny name,
The Sagrada Family something or other .
I've got it, well not it,
No, a postcard, from my ex
Unfinished really (not my ex he's finished)
A bit of a building site not like ours
No, not like ours...
Here are the felt tips and
For those of you who aren't allowed felt tips
Because of the spontaneous graffiti project
workshop we had in last week and the incident in
the corridor, washable pens and crayons.
Now then pay attention
we are here to learn something.
Let's imagine what colours Picasso used
In colouring in his famous painting, *Guernica.*
Obviously it's about War
And War as you will all know is a bad thing
And none of you must start one,
Use lots of red and orange
Here is the blue in case
you want sky but we have run out of yellow
But that's okay because we don't need sunshine
today. Ignore the light bulb in the top left corner
of the picture let's pretend it's not switched on.

I will order more yellow soon.
Try not to draw both eyes on the side like Picasso
because it's silly and we don't look like that.

You don't need to know anything about art to
teach it, my boyfriend is a painter... and decorator
Last week we had fun and education
Joining the dot to dots
on *Starry, Starry Night* by Don McLean
And drawing alien arms
on the Venus Di Milo by Leonardo Di Caprio.

Now children, you see this man here
Impersonating *Edward Munch's The Scream*
He is our visitor today and he will teach you
Everything there is to know about poetry
He doesn't have a real job like me
And his name is Kevin.

The Lost Art of Catching Trains

'You learn from hobos
The art of catching trains'
(Rod McKuen)

Terminal,
These feelings,
Limping, crippled pigeons
Pecking at pasty crusts.
Under Victorian
Raised eyebrows.

Written on time and tagged
onto the railway embankment,
Inch"
Size has meaning;
every shudder of graffiti,
a body falling into electricity.

Pushing myself to the platform's edge,
closing my eyes, feeling for raised
warning circles through my soles
as we hurtle in foetal chairs out
of this particular auricle of darkness

over river on rivet and metal.
or swaying like bruised fruit,
ready to drop, waiting for
green lights in our minds
and at our fingers.
Control is given to us;
a relieved sigh as doors part.

an exchange of audiences
a ticket to deride
platform shoes
ho ho ho
By a less than grand Central Station

I sat down and wept for
the lost art of catching trains
and letting them go.

An Apoplexy For Poetry

To begin at the beginning... again
Neither Llareggub nor Terry Street,
Dismal in fasting November,
Rain edges its way down uncleaned glass.
a cat has piled the executed at the front door,
weathered windows cover vision with fog
blurred houses become watercolours.

The see saw of passing sirens
in the city of dog the cats claw .
Neither Peru nor Benidorm
the cultural rot does not concern
the girls who trot the well worn trail
from Cooperage to Est est est
and all the shots fired between.

The candyman's trumpet farts
a fanfare for ghosts and grails
long since rotten on hooks.
Neither tenor bull nor jingling geordie.
the concerns of the literati
De situ septic tankus
and sanctorum bollocks.

Primum cantauit Caedmon
out of tune and out of Durham
where Caddell's bonsai'd work grew.
Neither Guttersnipe
nor the booted Prince of Sparty Lea.
made a single dent in
the armour of hegemony.

As clear as Crystal
The Liar boys turn the earth
rake up reality and the fluvial suspects,
Neither Ultima Thule
nor Eric's axe though sharp

cuts through the great
British indifference.

We are lost
purveyors of cack
local poets and tribal chieftains;
at war with 'the establishment'
but mostly with ourselves.
It is a principle we hold most dear
biting the hand that keeps us in beer.

Empire builders
from the Tyne to the Tees,
and the Wear to the Tweed,
Neither King Ida's Watchchain,
Silken Stand nor Mudfog's attrition.
The passwords for success
are naked and ambition.

New words in their order
and the jukebox plays the bear
Rat arsed in the Crown Posada
Where every poet has an M.A.,
The Iron man in Cullercoats
has wed the Angel of the North,
Fundamental changes alter
the substance of the source.

Runic torches splay and arc
across the Tees Valley,
Pissing where Ginsberg pissed
howling dark in rats alley.
Where smokestack flares
old ideals of underdog menace
reclaiming our tradition
The bards of Vane terrace?

The room was blue
with vagary and about to implode
words kicking at the heels
of Horace's epodes,

dunshing like easter eggs
at Christ knows who's tomb.
We are the weather forecasters
Of poetic doom.

And the Vandals only reached the door
And chalked their names in lightly
Crushed by the great indifference
Court Jesters of the Muse Almighty.
The sheep are spelling out the names
Of those tipped for posterity.
The dye runs down their fleeces
And robs us of all clarity.

The great the good,
The ear of wood,
The brave, the bold,
The ones whose souls
Were all but sold
For Acne gold.
Left in the cold
as foretold.

To end at the end and seek to stand
Our boots in this acknowledged land
We are rutting in the trough of shit
For a mouthful of the holy tit.
The work-shopped out
The nothing to say
All queue to fight
For equal pay.

Bunting's ghost at Swan Hunter's gate
Beleaguered by the Welfare State
Where poets sign the dotted line
For a chance to sell their pearls to swine.

An apoplexy for poesy
A fait accompli for no one knows
And beyond it, the deep blue air, that shows
Nothing but the raucous cackle of crows.

This Tyne

the gramophone in the Crown Posada
scratches out George Formby
whose wife never let kiss his leading ladies,
but I would kiss you.
We drift along the quayside like untethered boats
touching, barging, jostling ,
Your faith is unsinkable.
We are slow mourners
heads low up Dog Leap Stairs
pausing to forget to kiss
under the viaducts at Castle Keep
and deep into the day and into our pockets
we drink in one corner
or another of The Bridge Hotel.
This Tyne that flows like ale over dreamers.

I am waiting for
unrequited love at Central Station
It is a train that never stops arriving.
Her text is enigmatic she is tardy
a word I found in 'O' level *Lear*
but almost appropriate here
in the tiled splendour of the Centurion.
she drives my bonnie dreams away
I keep my feet as still as bed linen
My heart is happy through the night.

Victoria Regina sits looking
up the skirts on the Bigg Market
from her throne outside of St.Nicks,
no Alberts in sight
but plenty of Tom, Dicks and Debbies.
From bar to bar to bar,
searching for a taste of what we are,
and love is kebab cheap
or brief in the darkness
of a hire purchased car.

and the fog on the Tyne is
a timeshare investment.

The girl in the Windows arcade is singing Verdi.
the poets huddle in the Tower behind the Gate
Newcastle is no longer just a city of starlings.
Morrissey mentioned Skipsey at the City Hall
lost on his disciples, apostles of the shopping mall.

I am drinking cooking lager in the Crown Posada
Listening to George Formby,
whose leading ladies were never kissed
Evangelists and minstrels merge at Monument,
The clear white light looks blue.
Grainger Town is about to cast off
its concrete overcoat and dance.
Naked as the Baltic, the Sage's mirrored snail.

This Tyne, from now
until forever running
Between you and me.

The Lost Boys

for Aidan Halpin

We must learn to hold it together
accept our inability to be charming,
accept the girth of our wit is proportionate
to half the girth of our waistlines,
accept this riposte from the latest
barmaid as par,
accept that calling her a barmaid may
have queered the pitch
accept that our terminology is due for revision,
accept that the 'kids on the street'
are our children or worse our children's children.
Learn that growing old disgracefully
is a synonym for growing old ridiculously,
Learn to shrug at ageism
Learn to adopt the mannerisms of those
we mocked when we were the enfant terrible
and learn that we were as inane and banal
as the current 'enfant terrible'.
We will grow to be lost if we do not,
and Peter Pan although the world's role model
is as lost as us and twice as scared.
We will grow wise and wear slippers with zips,
We will grow water bottles in our beds
We will grow ear and nasal hair
We will grow up into our parents
and these young bastards with no respect
have got it coming to them and
serve them right.
We will grow the nerve to move to
the first person;
I will grow and accept and learn
although I have decided never to stoop
so low as to validate my love for the lost
boys that have come and gone.

There are Loads of Planets with a North

It doesn't make me a hero,
or an alien doctor from the BBC
It's just a part of what I am
and a part of who I claim to be,
Time and relative distance
in space from the naughty north
to the sexy south and all this
is relative to where you are
of course.

There are loads of planets with a north

And I live in the south to the Scots
who espouse that I'm just English
and there is no difference and borderline's
are arbitrary and part of this condition
In Lapland they would laugh in the face of a
Glaswegian (stupidly)
if they said they were northern
and geography is the rules
they teach you in school,
so assume the position.

There are loads of planets with a North

Just because you say something
doesn't make it so,
Turning the world upside
down exchanges one pole
for another pole,
From compass pointless arguments
about history and tradition
the London scene appoints its leaders
and they begin an expedition.
To teach us what we know inherently to be true
that labels like North and South
have got everything to do

with the landscape of redundant issues,
with the way you say your vowels
and they layer on the patronage
with linguistic whoops and howls.
There are lots of planets with a north
and just as many with a south
Some times it seems it's just a case of who
or maybe whom has the biggest mouth,
I would shout it from the rooftops
but I may be misunderstood
I could buy a whippet and a flat cap
they say it's in my blood
I have been flattening my vowels
like Chaucer did before me
If I talk in my own dialect
why do some people ignore me?

I am for richness, diversity
of speech and thought
Ignorance is only knowing your place,
poverty is a label that can't be bought
I am a product of years
of nurturing this industrial chip
on a shoulder meant for digging coal
and welding bits on ships
So what's the point in industry
when nothing is worth making
It's more than hard to tell a Charv
the can of worms he's waking
and that's a mixed metaphor
if I ever I saw one
I am standing at a crossroads
with my Novocastrian hard on
and Dr. Whoever and whatever
you say goes
but you couldn't catch a cold
with that elitist pose.

It doesn't make me a working class hero
to sigh as David Tennant

suppresses those rich Scots vowels
or him a traitor for his anglicised speeches.
I won't fight him on the beaches
Or castigate linguistic teachers
Or take the piss out of North East creatures
For covering the deck chair
of the Queen's English
With an indecipherable dialect towel.
There are lots of planets with a North
To misquote the Doctor as this poem aborts.
You can take the man out of the language
But not the language out of the man.

What are we afraid of?
What are parochialists after,
For Charver read chav,
for laffter read laughter.
I digress as words run their course
Dicks for Dictionaries,
Encyclopaedophiles,
Pedants and much worse,
fuck it
There are loads of planets with a North.
Why aye!

Dances with Vowels

If I had known that *Vowels*
Was an anagram of *Wolves*
Or indeed that *Wolves* was an anagram of *Vowels*
I would have written this a long time ago.

I was raised by a pack of vowels.
Five unrelated aunties
Who gathered around my crib
Reciting the incantation

Aaah
Eeee
Aye
Oh
You.

When I said crib there I wanted to say manger
That might mean I have a God Complex
An inner sublimated Christ rising to the surface
However I am an atheist
Which means I don't know if God exists
Not that I don't care if God exists,
I don't know what Jung would have said about that
Maybe he wouldn't care by now.
Jimmy Young would have said TTFN
An acronym devoid of vowels.

I love You

Has an awful lot of vowels
Except in Text messages
Where it simply says I LY.

If little red Riding Hood's Grandmother
Had been eaten by a vowel I suspect
It would be an 'e.'
I ate an 'e' once but that's a different poem.

I found a bag of consonants in my computer
Just rattling around, I tried to use them
Ffffffff Fffff Kkk
Swearing is rubbish without vowels.
I was raised by vowels

I speak the language
And flatten them like a carpenter making a cross.
My aunts are all dead now nailed into coffins
Howling like Werevowels.

Red Dalek's Love Song

You will promise to love, honour and obey,
We will marry on the home planet.
You will promise to obey,
We will happy that is an order
you will obey, you will obey
I will buy you a bungalow in Southwick
And you will exterminate all germs from our bungalow,
I will buy you Domestos from the supermarket
And many other cleaning utensils and kitchen appliances.
You will obey, you will obey.
I will sing your strange earth songs with you
Because I too want to have sex on the beach
Although I do not have a human member or
An orifice for lager.
I will be a techno dalek,
I will sing to you,
I've noticed you around
I find you very attractive
Will you… will you
Will you go to bed with me?
I have my own ramp.

Preamble

The birds were writing Hitchcock scripts
Under certainly cartoon clouds.
You gathered seaweed and tassled
Your handbag with its salt.

Puffins and Eider ducks bobbed,
A boat trip a season too early.
A precious link your hand
Through my arm and I
Still love you, although I
Would never be careless
Enough to let you know.

Your heart as usual elsewhere
And mine as usual, a wreck
Seaweed strewn, drying out
As tides change.

Occupied Territory

And that was all it was a grief stricken heart pinned on a six
        inch nail
And they said write this and write that and we will buy you off
This system has never been known to fail.
Give us any anger you might have at 'so called injustices' and we
        will
Give you a carpet to sweep them under,
Give you an expensive light-shade to cover the glare of that bare
        light-bulb,
We will train you to do the tricks you need to do, when to howl
And when to keep your mouth shut, when to beg and when to
        wait.
Show you how to recognise the hand that feeds you
Show you how to act in public
Show you what to say in our meetings.
Show you what you need to sacrifice and who not whom
And we will never call you a collaborator
We will never bother you with the old fashioned agendas
Of the left, after all what is left of the left?
We will show you how to be right
We will show you how to be right for us.

In occupied territory the poets are colonists not liberators
Suppressants not anti-depressants,
They come to feed at the oasis, drawn by clear water
And the promise of easy pickings.
(Hey at least he's not bitter)
What on earth would we have to be bitter about?
Us regional types.
Shepherded to pens by wolf-trainers.
In occupied territory the class lines are drawn
You must learn the lessons of humility and humus
You must learn that crudités are raw root vegetables and not
        swear words,
You must learn that all you believe in must be watered down
Must become a stock for the soup that you will be pedalling.
Don't ask me how I know this,

I exchanged dinner for lunch years ago,
Accepted the duvet over the continental quilt
The lounge over the living room
I have been sleeping with the enemy
Too long to remember.
What the world was like before Garden Centres
And home make over programmes gave me my opinions.

Some days I know ,
I am my own worst enemy.
Other days I want to be.

A Threshold Too Far

You say I want us to hold hands
while we cross the Charles Bridge
I am inside me
You had taken your clothes off
It was your birthday.

Tomorrow I will wander Prague alone
Take photos of a shop full of bright Russian Dolls
For my daughter's eyes only.
I flick through them for you
As a rehearsal of solidarity.

This city was built where a man was digging
The exit to a house,
because even a noble man
May stumble over a threshold.

You tell me of a dream
Of a live fox in your womb and mouth,
I witness the loss of something
As I drive on a road listening
To a banal radio station
To hear you speak in traffic.

Tomorrow I will tell you how scared I am of bridges.
You will be the architect building a storm of words.

Driving to the Same Houses

I keep driving to the same houses
As if I have left something,
Deliberately, as if it is time to collect something.
Now when the fences are down
And the dogs unleashed.

This house is a bad caricature
Of my memory, it has put on weight
In the form of a conservatory,
It has faded slightly at its edges
From use.
I sit outside in the car
Where the strangers now live
Moving the ornaments
In my mind.
The children play on the streets
But I am not visible in their world.

I drive to my Mother's house
And look at the sepia vertical blinds
Wish she would make them twitch again
And then
Coffee and news
Time swept away
Like digestive crumbs.

I Am Not a Stone

On Marsden Beach
Throwing stone after stone
But I expect to connect nothing.
You text me,
I tell you where I am
You arrive inappropriately shod
Stumbling over pebbles.
Throwing stone after stone,
I find a piece of soft slate
And write my name
On a pebble,
Throw that too,
The sea makes a show
Of ignoring it.
You ask me to write
Your name on a pebble,
Which you throw.
The sea breathes in and out
Indifferent,
Rolling stones after stone,
Not looking for any single stone,
Just knowing them all.
I continue throwing stones,
You talk some more,
A poem already forming
In your head.
But I was in my moment
Like the sea knowing
stone after stone
and sometimes
though you choose
different, a stone
is just a stone.

The Times When I'd Rather Not Be in the Room and the Times When I Would

When poetry is wearing its self important head
and leaves you to wonder what is the point and
Wishing for a rocket launcher to level the area.

When poetry has its *voice* on, that drones and leaves
You empty as an aircraft hangar during the blitz
And you would give anything for realism and for
Charles Bukowski to be alive so you could drink
Him under his fable.

When poetry leaves that self satisfied, smug glow
As it describes yet again the various shenanigans
Of flowers and the way the sunlight falls on something
Out of context and dull as dishcloths.

When poetry is wearing its pretentious head and banging
On about silence and the way nothing means everything,
There are some things that don't need explaining
Like air and breathing , it is better not to think about it
In case we lose the beat and air invisible evades us.

When poetry is young and roars loudly about injustice
But has no solutions only polemic sabres and the usual
Happens as we attempt to shout down injustice,
Another injustice arrives and sneaks in another way
Whilst the focus is on the first injustice.

When poetry is brave and beautiful, rendering silence
Silent. Telling us what we don't necessarily want to hear
And telling us in such a way that passionately
is the only way we can care and we step out of ourselves
for one spliced second and touch vestigial wings.

When poets make themselves human and forget about
Their responsibilities whilst bearing full responsibility
For their art, for their *crafty sullen art.*

When poets narrow their vision and fall prey to self obsession
And fall to tai chi-ing in fields where bullocks wait to die
And become introspective to the point of telling us all about
Their shopping lists and hobbies as if being a poet with hobbies
Makes them more important than a member of the public with
      hobbies.
When poets rescind their membership like that it boils my
      lymphatic fluid.

Oh look what I just did , hoisted on my own, fallen on my sabre
I take full responsibility for being obscure, obtuse and obligated
To the fraternity, the big dumb ox-ford dictionary caught in the
Teeth of a Thesaurus Rex as it rips its throat out, its gullet out,
      its oesophagus out
Its front neck, its windpipe, its …oh you get the idea!

When poetry explains itself as if we are brain dead.

When poetry is more than you ever thought it could be.

Acknowledgements

Thank you to Deborah Murray, Anita Govan, Nancy Somerville, Sheila Wakefield, Colin Donati, James Oates, Steve Urwin, The Hardly Boys, Crista Ermiya, Bram Gieben, Robin Cairns, Kath Kenny, Kate Fox, Peter Mortimer, Kitty Fitzgerald, Fatma Stanners, Trevor Bentley, Hazel Mollison, Aidan Halpin and Andy Croft, for many diverse reasons.

These poems were first published in the following publications by Kevin Cadwallender: *Eager for Fire* (Riot Publications, 1984), *Spider in the Bath* (with Trevor Bentley; Dancing Frog/Sacred Pig Publications, 1985), *Lifesong* (with John Cadwallender; Toerag, 1986), *And this is Fate* (with Joy Larraine; Toerag, 1986), *Son of Life Song* (with John Cadwallender; Hybrid, 1989), *Fairy Tales from the Supermarket* (Hybrid, 1990), *Hand Signals* (Hybrid, 1991), *The Frankincense* (with Dave Brown; Monster, Hybrid, 1991), *Heartbreak Hotel* (with Dave Brown; Hybrid, 1992), *The Last Great Northern Whale* (Rookbook Publications, 1992), *A Rumour of Tigers* (with Dave Brown, Dave Calder, Mike Dillon, Barry Graham, Jeff Lawson and John McCaughie; Blue Moon, 1993), *Baz Poems* (Rebel Inc, 1993), *Sons of Flint and Pitch* (with Dave Calder, Mike Dillon and Bob Shields; The Candyman's Trumpet, 1994), *Liquorice Root* (The Candyman's Trumpet, 1996), *Apatosaurus Bends* (The Candyman's Trumpet, 1996), *Quiet as the Rafters* (Blue Elephant, 1996), *Once Below a Time* (with Ted Smith-Orr; Wagga Moon, 1997), *The Captain's Log vols 1 and 2* (Hybrid, 1997), *Baptism* (with David B Calder; Attic Press, 1997), *The Dynamo Field* (Mackay Jack, 1997), *Hardly Literature* (with John McCaugie, Mike Dillon and Bob Shields; Rookbook, 1998), *Ugly Light* (The Publisher, 1998), *Views of Views* (Great North Forest, Tyne and Wear, 1999), *Public* (IRON Press, 2001), *The Word Lodge* (Silt, 2002), *one2five* (with David B Calder, Alistair Robinson, Kitty Fitzgerald and Tom Pickard; Durham County Council, 2002), *Voyages* (with Bridget Jones and Colin Hagan; Cleveland Arts, 2002), *Sundland* (Civic Society, 2003), *Baz Uber Alles* (dogeater, 2004), *Rewiring Houdini* (Bee, 2006), *The South Face of Groucho Marx* (with Aidan Halpin; Red Squirrel, forthcoming) and *Colouring in Guernica* (Red Squirrel, 2007).